Managing Big Feelings and Hidden Fears

A vital resource, this guide provides practical strategies to address children's anxieties about real and hidden issues. Intended for use with the accompanying storybook, *Who's Afraid of the Monster?*, which offers a child-friendly story in verse of a monster who nobody has seen or heard and a King who pretends to be brave but is very scared. This guide provides the theory behind and offers practical solutions to a variety of Big Feelings and Hidden Fears.

A companion guide for use by primary educators, support staff and all those working with children, the book is divided into three easy-to-follow parts. Part One presents the theory behind how and why Big Feelings in children arise and how Creative Art and Drama can help. Part Two contains activities and exercises with photocopiable/downloadable instructions, as well as a list of resources for each activity and guidelines for safe working. Part Three offers further activities and ways in which to exploit the story such as discussion points, plays and models.

Underpinned by substantiated theory into the stages of children's emotional development, it offers realistic solutions for parents, carers, teachers and classroom assistants who simply do not have the time or resources to attend to their children's very real but hard-to-verbalise fears.

Penny McFarlane works as a clinical supervisor and trainer for counsellors and arts therapists. Formerly a mainstream teacher, she qualified as a dramatherapist and then spent 25 years bringing dramatherapy into education. www.pennyannmcfarlane.com

Rebecca A. Jarvis graduated with a First Class BA(Hons) in Illustration at University of Plymouth, UK, where she also received the Dane Watkins Interactive Award. Her mixed media work focuses predominantly on hopeful imagery, especially useful during the current times. See more of Rebecca's work on her website: www.rajarvisstudios.co.uk

Managing Big Feelings and Hidden Fears

A Practical Guidebook for
'Who's Afraid of the Monster?'

PENNY MCFARLANE

ILLUSTRATED BY REBECCA A. JARVIS

Routledge
Taylor & Francis Group

LONDON AND NEW YORK

Designed cover image: Rebecca A. Jarvis

First published 2024
by Routledge
4 Park Square, Milton Park, Abingdon, Oxon OX14 4RN

and by Routledge
605 Third Avenue, New York, NY 10158

Routledge is an imprint of the Taylor & Francis Group, an informa business

British Library Cataloguing-in-Publication Data
A catalogue record for this book is available from the British Library

Library of Congress Cataloging-in-Publication Data
Names: McFarlane, Penny, author. | Jarvis, Rebecca (Illustrator),
illustrator. | McFarlane, Penny. Who's afraid of the monster
Title: Managing big feelings and hidden fears: a practical guidebook for 'who's afraid of the monster?' / Penny McFarlane; illustrated by Rebecca Jarvis.
Description: 1st edition. | New York: Routledge, 2023. |
Includes bibliographical references. |
Summary: – Provided by publisher.
Identifiers: LCCN 2022055412 (print) | LCCN 2022055413 (ebook) |
ISBN 9781032478944 (pbk) | ISBN 9781003386414 (ebk)
Subjects: LCSH: Storytelling. | Anxiety in children. | Fear in children. |
Stress management for children. | Storytelling in education.
Classification: LCC LB1042 .M337 2023 (print) | LCC LB1042 (ebook) |
DDC 370.15/34–dc23/eng/20230313
LC record available at https://lccn.loc.gov/2022055412
LC ebook record available at https://lccn.loc.gov/2022055413

ISBN: 978-1-032-47894-4 (pbk)
ISBN: 978-1-003-38641-4 (ebk)

DOI: 10.4324/9781003386414

Typeset in VAG Rounded Std
by Deanta Global Publishing Services, Chennai, India

Access the support material: https://resourcecentre.routledge.com/speechmark

For all children everywhere
And the child in all of us

Contents

Contents

Figures

Introduction

Welcome to the guidebook on Managing Big Feelings and Hidden Fears.

This resource aims to provide simple theory as to how and why children experience such overwhelming feelings as well as useful Creative Art and Drama activities and exercises on how to manage them.

This guidebook, as well as the accompanying storybook, has been written with teachers, parents and primary carers of young children in mind and, as such, uses layman's terms with easy-to-follow information and instructions.

The aim is to provide a handy resource which will empower those who are trying to support children whose, often unidentifiable, feelings threaten to engulf them.

PART ONE

As well as an exploration into 'Why this book now?' and an explanation of 'How to use this book', Part One presents the theory behind how and why Big Feelings in children arise and why Creative Art and Drama techniques work better with small children than Talking Therapies.

PART TWO

Contains activities and exercises with photocopiable/downloadable instructions. A list of resources for each activity as well as guidelines for safe working are also given.

PART THREE

Offers further activities and ways in which to exploit the story such as discussion points, plays, models etc.

Part One

Why this book now?

In the wake of the Covid 19 pandemic and with the current and ever-increasing global anxiety about such things as climate change, the world is experiencing a mental health tsunami, the impact of which is being felt most keenly by the young. In January 2021 the Kelleher (2021) reported that "The number of children looking for psychiatric help for mental health issues soared when the lockdown restrictions were lifted last summer".

Compounding this, there has been a rise in parental separation and domestic violence; the ensuing effect of which has resulted in many young children suffering from indefinable fears and general anxiety (Bradbury-Jones and Isham 2020)

The main, underlying message of this book is, as the King in the story says,

> "What we don't see and what we don't hear
> Just makes us more frightened, it builds up the Fear"

Both the pandemic and climate change are things "we don't see or hear"; they are not tangible and, as such, are difficult concepts for younger children to grasp. Likewise, a general atmosphere of tension in a household during or following a domestic upheaval can be anxiety provoking for a child even if there is no violence. Situations such as these build up vague, undefinable feelings of dread and fear.

Giving a shape to a name and a structure to a feeling can help children bring the uncontrollable under control. The overarching message of the storybook, as given through metaphor and the activities outlined in Parts Two and Three of this guidebook, is geared towards giving shape, structure and therefore control over these vague, indefinable emotions.

How to use this book

There are many ways to use both the storybook and/or the guidebook, depending on whether you are a parent or carer wishing to calm your child's anxiety through reading

DOI: 10.4324/9781003386414-1

a quirky, humorous bedtime story and trying out some of the simple activities, or a teacher wishing to address the emotional literacy and therefore resilience of your class.

The story stands alone. With its metaphor of a King who pretends to be brave but is really very scared and a Monster who, despite never having been seen, terrorises the people, the story brings across the message that it's better to face up to our fears, talk about them and find ways to address them. In other words, externalise them rather than internalise and suffer.

The story mentions some of the activities and these, and further activities, are summarised in The Big Feelings List that can be found in Part Two. This List will aid children in remembering the activities and enables them to tick them off once they've practised them.

It is advisable to read Part One of the guidebook prior to trying out the activities since this gives

- The theory behind the use of metaphor through Creative Drama and Art activities as a way of helping children externalise their feelings.

- An explanation as to what happens in children's brains that results in overwhelming feelings.

- A brief summary of the stages of emotional development as an aid to understanding which activity is best suited to each child or class of children.

- Some general advice and tips to help children manage Big Feelings.

- Gives advice on how to recognise more severe scenarios and how to react to them.

- A brief look at how to manage yourself.

- The reason why abstract fear may be as, and in some cases, more frightening for young children than something they can identify.

- A description of the importance of witnessing and the use of ritual in helping to normalise Big Feelings.

- A list of useful resources.

Following on from Part One, the activities in Part Two can be used in any order, although a mixture of breathing, mime and drawing/writing works best especially if the committing to paper is the final exercise since this consolidates in concrete form the lessons learnt through the previous practices. It is suggested therefore that the photocopiable/downloadable sheets are used at the end of the sessions, after the activity, as a way of further calming and controlling the feelings. Colouring in the diagrams can be a final, soothing exercise.

The activities are grouped around the Big Feelings of anger and anxiety/worry/fear for ease of referral, although obviously many of the exercises are applicable to a mixture of feelings. A short explanation is given at the beginning of each group of exercises. Most of the activities can be used on an individual, small group or class basis. It is perhaps worth remembering that there is great empowerment in being witnessed as well as in the use of ritual (see Part One: Externalising and witnessing).

Part Three lists ways in which the story can be explored through enactment and, with slightly older children, how the roles of the King, Mouse, Boy, Monster and People can be taken on to provide a way of understanding, witnessing and normalising feelings of guilt, shame, fear, anxiety, courage, bravery, despair, hope and relief.

Resources and materials

All the activities require few or no resources. A general kit bag would be as follows:

- Coloured pens or pencils of some sort.

- Paper and card.

- Scissors.

- Sticky notes for the volcano activity.

- A roll of wallpaper (for use on the reverse side).

- Lengths (at least a metre square) of coloured material.

- Various chairs and cushions.

- Dressing-up clothes to make the acting more fun; these are not obligatory since, with a little imagination, it is surprising what can be done with the lengths of material (see Part Three: Material).

Why Creative Art and Drama activities?

Very young children are not always able to express their feelings in words. Instead, they are much more inclined to choose the medium of play and expressive behaviour to externalise their emotions. Historically, there has been a tendency within support agencies to locate the problem in a child's 'acting in' or acting out' rather than look at the issue at the root of this behaviour. However, if a young child cannot tell you what their issue is, then how do you find out? Counsellors and therapists who use creative arts methods – for example, talking through a puppet, role playing, or using small figures to tell stories – are much more likely, not only to get to the root of the problem but to get there faster since their methods contain an element of fun, which helps to build the component of trust necessary in any therapeutic alliance.

For example, although an older child may be able to tell you that their mother is suffering from depression and is unable to communicate with them, a younger child can only show you through the medium of their play that the baby tiger can't reach the Mummy tiger because there is a great big dragon in the way. Thus, we find in fairy tales that Goodness is personified by the beautiful princess, Magic by the fairy godmother and Evil by the wicked witch.

In his Theory the developmental psychologist and philosopher Jean Piaget explained that children under a certain age find it very difficult to process abstract ideas (Piaget 1970). As an example, trying to explain the concept of death to a small child can prove problematical and sometimes well-meaning parents will try to find some euphonism which is more comfortable, both to them and the child. Using an explanation such as "she's asleep" or "they've gone on a journey" often results, however, in the child being scared to go to sleep or go on a journey themself. Therefore, the best way to explain the concept of death to a small child is to let them see a dead bird or perhaps a pet when it dies. Equally, watching the changes in the seasons by seeing what happens to a tree for example, can be supportive.

This inability to process abstract ideas can also be demonstrated when a young child is angry or anxious. They cannot always tell you why they are, only that they have this Big Feeling inside that feels like it is going to burst out of them. Using Creative Art and Drama activities bypasses the 'why' of the situation, avoids the 'let's talk about it' and goes straight into meeting the issue somatically, ie using body, breath and visualisation. So, we 'burst' out like a volcano, become a warrior to meet our fears and let our breath out in short bursts as we visualise a saucepan letting off steam.

This inability to explain feelings is made even more impossible if there is no obvious situation from which the feelings may have arisen. In general, children are much more aware of how their parents are feeling than the parents give them credit for. "Sometimes children's 'bad' behaviour, anger or even violence can mask a parent's problems, allowing the focus of shame to shift from parent to child in a concealed transaction that neither may be fully conscious of" (Chown 2013: 180).

The value of metaphor

We have discussed how young children find it difficult to express their worries or anger in words and often prefer to use the expressive arts to convey their feelings. This section provides a short explanation as to why this happens.

To solve a problem in a creative way, two phases corresponding to the two modes of the brain are necessary. Firstly, the problem is 'felt' by the creative, perceptive right brain responsible for parallel processing and spatial/depth recognition. The person, child or adult, 'feels' that there is something wrong before understanding what it might be. (Interestingly, since the right side of the brain governs the left side of the body and vice versa, the heart, the so-called seat of the emotions, is found mostly on the left side of the body.) This problem, however, needs to be understood by the logical, reasoning, analytical left brain, which is responsible for ordering speech and language. Metaphor can be used to facilitate this procedure. From the Greek *meta* meaning 'across' and *phor* 'to carry', metaphor carries across or transfers images which may be emotionally based from the right brain to the left brain where they can be given meaning through language.

The effectiveness of using art or drama as a way of facilitating this procedure is therefore self-explanatory as it is a "procedure that moves from talking to creative action where the client is encouraged to let go, play in space, integrate action, imagination, feeling, thought" (Casson 1998: 13). Metaphor, therefore can be seen as a bridge between the world of fiction and fact, of fantasy and reality, of emotion and understanding.

What happens in children's brains

Big Feelings are rarely initially understood by children and often not by adults either. His sister switching off the television, when it should have been his turn to do so, sends Jake into a fit of uncontrollable rage from which he has to learn to calm down and manage. He doesn't understand why this simple action has this effect on him and in addition to his anger, he then has to deal with the shame that he has reacted in this way. Jake comes from a calm, rational, emotionally literate family so he is learning fast how to control these outbursts. Other children, however, are not so lucky.

We all possess, not one, but three brains: the higher, or rational brain, the lower, mammalian or emotional brain and the primitive, most ancient reptilian brain. At birth, a child's higher brain is unfinished and for a few years it is the lower brain which will be calling the shots. Because the higher brain, responsible for problem solving, for reasoning and reflection, for kindness, empathy and concern is still undeveloped, the emotional systems and primitive impulses belonging to the mammalian and reptilian brains will dominate, and at times all too easily overwhelm the child. Powerful bursts of rage and harmful behaviour will often ensue to the intense distress of both child and adult. However, it is important here to recognise that this is not about being naughty but rather due to having an immature infant brain, whose distress systems have already been set up at birth to ensure the infant's survival.

Certain chemicals in the child's brain will also affect his behaviour. Oxytocin and opioids (the feel-good factors) are produced when a child is held, nurtured and receives love and attention but are blocked by the absence of these behaviours, creating a kind of hormonal hell for the child concerned. Additionally, an important alarm system in the lower brain, the amygdala, will action the release of stress hormones if it feels threatened. These hormones are needed to prepare the body for survival, for fight or flight mode, but if the child has not been helped by calmness and comfort to develop their higher brain and manage their Big Feelings of frustration, rage or distress then these stress hormones will be pumped out again and again. Eventually the child's brain will become accustomed to high levels of these chemicals – cortisol, adrenalin and noradrenalin – and they will feel they are continually living in an unsafe and unpredictable world.

Helping the child to manage Big Feelings is therefore paramount, not only for their distress in the moment but for their future. "A child's sense of being fundamentally unsafe in the world can become her way of knowing herself and other people" (Sunderland 2006: 29).

Helping the child manage Big Feelings

When a child learns to manage their big feelings through calm, constructive support, neurological pathways are formed between the higher and lower brains. The higher brain will then eventually start to control the primitive impulses and reactions of rage and fear and this will lead to effective management of these destructive emotions. A child can then be helped to think about what they are feeling and find ways of discharging or assimilating the powerful energy that is being created.

How to manage more severe scenarios

In most cases this energy dissipates naturally following an intervention from a calm and controlled adult. Yet, repeated behaviour that gives cause for concern and may need a referral to children's mental health services may include the following:

- A sudden switch to agitated and occasionally repetitive action, often accompanied by a rise in temperature and/or sweating.

- Staring or unfocused eyes sometimes darting from side to side.

- A feeling that the child is 'not himself' and is unaware of what he is doing.

- A repeated regression to behaving at a much younger age, for example a toddler or baby, accompanied by frenzied actions and focused concentration over a period of time as if the child is remembering something.

If a child exhibiting the above behaviour needs to be contained in the absence of professional help, then the following may be helpful:

- Keeping the child physically safe is paramount as in making sure they cannot escape from the room and keeping all sharp objects out of reach.

- Keeping your voice calm and controlled at all times and repeating that the child is safe right here, right now in this room.

- Encouraging the child to enter into a game or state of play that involves some sense of rhythm and/or rime. Songs that involve clapping or rocking are useful here.

- Avoiding the temptation to enter into any fantasy or enactment with the child. (This is the province of professional therapeutic intervention.)

- Avoiding the 'triggers' to the outbursts as far as is possible and creating a consistently secure, familiar environment which may include the designation of one particular member of staff who has the child's trust.

- Once the child is calmer, breathing activities, such as those mentioned in Part Two, for example the *Golden String Breathing* activity, may be effective.

All of the above are useful strategies to help calm any child, whether or not there is cause for concern and referral to professional agencies. Additionally, the following points are worth taking into consideration.

How do you manage yourself?

It is especially important to remain calm when faced with a child who has 'lost it'. It is easy to descend into mirror behaviour, becoming another child and having a tantrum yourself because you 'can't deal with this right now'. I have, on occasion, listened to an adult trying to deal with an angry child and observed how their tone of voice is no different from that of the child itself. Taking a few moments to breathe deeply, to do a tension release, such as a breathing exercise (see Part Two), to remind yourself that you are the adult here and that the child is only trying to deal with the feelings which are threatening to overwhelm them, rather than seeking to be naughty, is time worth spent. The child needs to know that there is someone there for them who can hold these Big Feelings and who can return their world to one of safety and control. The following may be useful here:

- Meet your child's needs on an appropriate level which matches their level of intensity. For example, say "I can see how sad/angry/scared you are right now and that's a really big thing to be dealing with. I'm right here and I'm big enough to hold those big feelings". Maintain eye contact, coming down to their level if necessary.

- Pick your battles but be consistent in your boundaries. Avoid fighting over the things that really do not matter, always remembering that the child is just trying to find out how things work in the adult world and needs to have some sense of self within it. Avoid the trap of "If you do ..., I will/won't", since this threat or promise needs to be carried out or the child won't believe you again.

- Avoid pleading or arguing. Being clear, even if it seems to escalate the situation in the short term, is a better message to give the child since it also gives them the sense that the world is one with boundaries and they can feel safe within it.

- Physical soothing after the outburst, if appropriate, is the best way to encourage the re-emergence of those feelgood hormones which restore the child to calmness and security.

Stages of emotional development

In order to understand which activities are more appropriate for different age groups, it is worth giving a brief description of the stages of emotional development as outlined by psychological theorists J. Piaget (1970) and E.H. Erikson (1959) and the way that the Creative Expressive Model of dramatherapy as invented by Sue Jennings (Cattanach 1994) corresponds to and exploits these theories. During my time as a dramatherapist working with children in schools I have based much of my work on this Creative

Expressive Model since I have found that it offers the most effective methods of therapeutic intervention closely aligned to psychological theory.

The stages of the model, described as Embodiment, Projection and Role, tie in roughly to the three stages of emotional development as shown below.

Jennings	Piaget	Erikson
Embodiment	Sensory/motor	Trust versus Mistrust
Projection	Self and others	Industry versus Inadequacy
Role	Self as others	Identity versus Role

This is a vast oversimplification but its value lies in how it applies to the use of the creative arts in building emotional resilience as follows:

- During the Embodiment stage which corresponds approximately to 0 to 2 years, a child is only concerned with itself. Sensory activities, such as messy play, bubble blowing, finger painting, clay work etc are appropriate here.

- During the Projection stage (approximately 2 to 7 years) a child becomes aware that there is a world outside and begins to project their thoughts and feelings on to puppets, soft toys etc. This stage is the one most favoured by this guidebook since it emphasises the importance of externalising the Big Feelings rather than keeping them bottled up (see Part One: Witnessing and externalising).

- Finally, from about the age of 7 (although for many children this is much earlier) children acquire the ability to take on role. Piaget maintains that they are able to see themselves as others see them and Erikson stresses the importance of discovering identity and the roles available in society.

It is important to note here that we are dealing with emotional rather than chronological age. If a child has experienced some sort of trauma, abuse or even significant event such as a bereavement in the family or the arrival of a new sibling then their emotional development may be delayed and they may be functioning at a much younger age. As a children's therapist I often ask myself the question, "If I didn't know this child's age, how old would their behaviour be telling me they are?" Very often they will be presenting at the age at which the significant event happened. As a therapist it would then be necessary to go back to the emotional age at which the child is presenting and allow them to work (or play) through this unfinished process until it is time for them to move on.

For the purposes of this guidebook therefore, it can be seen from the above brief description that most of the activities relate to the Projection Stage. Part Three, however, does touch on the Role Stage and gives some ideas for further exploiting the story and includes suggestions which involve role play. But, as we have discussed, not every child is at the stage of emotional development where they are able to take on role and it is worthwhile considering this before doing any enactment. Those exercises which involve mime and bodywork relate more to the Embodiment/Sensory stage and are useful for a child of any age.

More information regarding these stages and their relation to the creative arts can be found in *Dramatherapy: Developing Emotional Resilience* (McFarlane 2005) and *Creative Drama for Emotional Support* (McFarlane 2012)

Emotional development and abstract fear

As has been explained, children under a certain age (and we are speaking here of emotional rather than chronological age) find it difficult to process abstract ideas. Thus, as carers or teachers of children, we are encouraged not just to talk about good and bad behaviour but to say "Let's see if you can sit quietly on the mat while I read this story". Being concrete, having tangible outcomes, helps the child understand exactly what is happening and what is being required of them. Drawing out what will happen in the future, for example when Mummy goes into hospital to have her baby, can often allay the older sibling's fears over this intangible future event that everyone is talking about.

Young children live in the world of make believe through which they learn "to explore the intricate and infinite complexities of life" (McFarlane 2012: 17). And usually, they have a very good grasp of where fantasy ends and reality begins. As Professor Mooli Lahad, Israeli psychologist and psychodrama specialist says, a child will happily trot or gallop on his pretend chair horse but will be very scornful if the parents try to feed it (Lahad 2000: 12). Unfortunately, some children are not encouraged in this healthy playacting, are given too many conflicting messages and/or are subjected to witnessing violence, whether real, or fantasy through films etc. As the King in the story says "What we can't see or hear just builds up the Fear", so the gaps in what the child cannot see or hear are filled in by imagination. When this indefinable Fear is great enough, any child, even with good parenting, may become overwhelmed by their inability to distinguish fact from fantasy (see Part Two: The pink and blue room). Thus, the intangible quality of anxiety, depression, fear, frustration pervading a household in the wake of a pandemic, a global event or, nearer to home, domestic violence or a bereavement, may leave a child filling in the gaps from what they are told with their own huge, imaginary fears. As a child my husband came downstairs screaming "The Budgie is going to get me, the Budgie is going to get me", after his parents had been watching news of the Budget on the television.

Externalising and witnessing

The effectiveness of the activities described in Part Two is due to the extent to which the child is able to externalise their Big Feelings and be witnessed while doing so. Whether through mime, projection through a puppet or some role play, the child will be allowing their feelings to surface, be processed and witnessed by a safe adult, thus giving the message that it is OK to be feeling this: that this is, in fact, normal.

An attitude on the part of the teacher or carer of positive, non-judgmental regard is therefore paramount. In this way the child will feel emboldened to be themself and to display their hopes and fears which, in turn, will be accepted and therefore given value by the witness.

If possible, it is preferable to keep any value judgments out of individual observations. A more useful approach might be simply to comment on what is happening; for example "I can see that your balloon has a lot of anger in it" or "Jake is showing us that his breath is stretching right out over the fields". Even a positive comment, by implication, if not given the next time, could convey the message of failure. An exception to this, is of course, praising the whole group, especially if the activity is not to be repeated.

As well as the teacher or carer there is value in the group as a whole playing the part of the witness. Especially with older children, for those that are able to take on role (see Part One: Stages of Emotional Development), dividing a class into smaller groups and having each group witness the others as they perform a play or other group activity is enormously empowering for the children concerned. This is enhanced if the performance involves ritual in some way as in the repetition of a particular action which is important or integral to the story.

The importance of ritual

For children who experience many changes, and indeed, childhood itself is a time of change, there is a need for structure and, therefore, safety in their lives. This structure can be created by ritual: the ritual of performing a well-known song or rhyme, the ritual of precursing a performance or activity by a familiar game or introduction exercise and, possibly most effectively, the ritual of allowing each child to repeat an important part of the story or activity while being witnessed by the others. Knowing what is going to happen creates an atmosphere of security and wellbeing which gives the child freedom to explore their emotions and develop an emotional literacy. Ideas and advice on facilitating effective and safe enactments are given in Part Three: Ideas for enactment.

Part Two

The Big Feelings List

1 The Magic Thumb
2 The Stepping Game
3 The Big Feelings/Happiness Box
4 Breathing activity: The Candle
5 Breathing activity: The Saucepan
6 Breathing activity: The Balloon
7 Mime: Robot/Doll
8 Mime: The Volcano
9 Discussion: The Volcano
10 Mime: Jack-in-the-Box
11 Drawing: The Angry Monster
12 Drawing/Writing: All About Me Book
13 Breathing activity: Golden String Breathing
14 Breathing activity: Belly Breathing
15 Pose: The Warrior
16 Pose: The Lion
17 Pose: The Tree
18 Drawing: Worry Doll/Puppet
19 Drawing/Collage: The Safe Place
20 Go Worry Rhyme
21 Storyboard: The Bad Dream
22 Discussion: The Pink and Blue Room

All of the above comprise a page giving details concerning the activity for the teacher, parent or guide, together with any resources needed and notes of caution if applicable. Where appropriate, photocopiable/downloadable pages with simple instructions for the child are also included and these are entitled *'My Candle Breathing'*, *'My Volcano'*, etc. Photocopiable/downloadable pictures to be coloured in, templates or blank pages are also offered for the child to consolidate the activity in a concrete form.

DOI: 10.4324/9781003386414-2

Assessment Activities

The following two activities are useful ways of finding out how a child is feeling generally and then of discovering what may be the cause behind their distress. As always, it's worthwhile remembering that a child may not be able to find the words to explain what they are feeling or why so a more creative approach may be needed. In these two activities the approach taken is in the form of a game.

The Magic Thumb

This activity can be used with children as young as three or four.

- Explain to the child that you have a 'magic thumb' and that when everything is good or happy, the thumb is straight up but when things are bad or unhappy, the thumb straight down.

- Start at the bottom and ask the child to shout 'STOP' when the thumb reaches where they are/how they are feeling.

- If the child shouts 'STOP' before the thumb reaches the top, ask them what would make the thumb go right up to the top.

(Quite often this results in a reply along the lines of '"If I had a new computer game", but occasionally a surprising and useful answer is revealed.)

The Stepping Game

This activity is best used with children from about five or six upwards who are able to relate their feelings to events.

- Explain to the child that you know that something is wrong for them and invite them to play a game with you to find out what. (Most children are intrigued enough to go along with this.)

- Say that you are going to make a guess as to what this 'wrong thing' has to do with; for example, school, friends, brother or sister, etc.

- Tell them that if you guess right, they have to take a step towards you but if you guess wrongly, they can take a step away from you.

- Make a few guesses which you know are not right so that the child can feel unthreatened and more in control of the game.

- Finally, and very gradually, make some more insightful guesses. (Do not push this; one or two steps towards you may be sufficient for you to then address the issue using a different activity.)

The Big Feelings/Happiness Box

As discussed (see Part One: Stages of Emotional Development), young children think in concrete rather than abstract terms. It is therefore a useful idea to construct a box or bin in a corner of the room which can hold all the Big Feelings once they have been let out or externalised. Any drawings that the children might produce, for example, from the *Golden String Breathing* (see Activities), can then go into this box for the safe keeping of the teacher, parent or carer who, it can be explained, is big and strong enough to hold all these feelings.

In the same way a Happiness Box can be constructed which can contain all the happy thoughts or ideas which make the children happy.

The boxes can be coloured or decorated in any way the children like.

Techniques used

The activities are based on a variety of techniques which have been proven successful in helping a child externalise and understand their Big Feelings. These techniques are:

breathing exercises, mime and bodywork, yoga poses, affirmations, visualisation, discussion, story work, play and performance, writing, drawing and art work.

Breathing activities

The effectiveness of using breathing to calm down is well known but what is sometimes overlooked is the fact that for young children, adding visualisation is paramount if they are going to use their breathing in a constructive way. This ties in with the aforementioned way in which young children can better understand if they are given a concrete example to explain an abstract thought (see Part One: Why Creative Art and Drama activities). Most of the breathing activities in this book are therefore accompanied by simple visualisations such as a candle or balloon which will help focus the child on the activity.

Mime and bodywork

Using mime helps a child make the link between their feelings and their body, and supports them in staying grounded during times of great stress. Being able to feel how the body is reacting to an emotion and managing to remain focussed in the body prevents the mind from spinning off into dissociation. Young children who have been exposed to undue amounts of stress or trauma sometimes need to revisit this stage of embodiment (see Part One: Stages of emotional development) before they can progress further in their emotional development.

Yoga poses

Three of the activities: *The Warrior, The Lion* and *The Tree* are taken from yoga because they have been found to be helpful in building confidence and emotional stability in children. Detailed instructions on how to perform these poses are given but more important than getting the pose absolutely right is the feeling that the body posture engenders. Asking questions such as "How do you feel when you are a lion/warrior/tree?" are therefore useful here.

Affirmations

Some of the activities such as *The Warrior* and *The Tree* poses are accompanied by the use of an affirmation. Affirmations should be positive and in the present tense, such as "I am strong, I am stable". Other activities may also lend themselves to affirmations such as "My worry is disappearing over the hills" in the *Golden String Breathing* and the child might like to be creative in thinking of others. Repetition of affirmations has been shown to forge new pathways in the brain and give rise to new ways of thinking, promoting self-confidence and self-belief.

Visualisation

There has been much research done into the positive effects of visualisation to the extent that it is a technique often used by Olympic athletes to attain their goals. "Visualisation helps top athletes to focus on the outcome in order to succeed" (Olympic Channel visualisation).

Additionally, as has already been explained in Part One: Why Creative Art and Drama activities?, visualising an activity they are engaged in is helpful for a young child and aids them in understanding abstract thoughts.

Discussion

Some of the activities, for example, *The Volcano*, lend themselves to discussion and examples of the way these can be exploited is given. Other activities, such as *The Worry Doll/Puppet* or *Golden String Breathing* have no suggestions for discussion but, depending on the age and ability of the children involved, would usefully lend themselves to discussions along the lines of "What worries you? Or what gives you butterflies in your tummy sometimes?"

Suggestions for discussion about the story are given in Part Three.

Story work

Children might be inspired to write their own stories about any of the activities listed below. As in *The Bad Dream* activity some children may prefer to create a storyboard or cartoon. Some useful prompts are:

- Who is the hero?
- What is he/she trying to do?
- What is the obstacle? What is stopping them?
- Who or what helps the hero?
- How do they get over the obstacles/difficulties?
- What happens in the end?

Play and performance

As we have discussed in Part One, play is the child's natural way of expression, and performance could be said to be 'witnessed play'. Any opportunity, therefore, to use play and performance in furthering any of the activities is a helpful and effective way to get the message across. Ideas for enactment are given in Part Three.

Drawing and art work

Putting things down on paper is a good way not only to calm a child after some other more energetic activity but also helps concretise the activity. For this reason, most of the activities include a 'colouring in' page which can serve to remind the child of the exercise. Additionally, older children can use their imaginations to draw their own pictures in such activities as *The Angry Monster, The Worry Doll/Puppet* or *My Safe Place* and keep their efforts to refer to later (in a Big Feelings/Happiness Box if you have one).

"If Big Feelings you've got, you can't hold 'em in.
But let 'em out safely, that way you will win."

Anger

We have all met the child who seems calm and controlled one minute and then erupts like an angry volcano the next, sometimes for no apparent reason. Something that is often overlooked is the fact that underneath all anger lies a sense of loss; whether this is the loss of a parent, sibling, favourite pet, toy or just a sense of self, the child feels that something has been taken away from them. Sometimes this sense of loss is more unidentifiable as, for instance, the loss of trust in a relationship, the loss of self-esteem when losing a game or the loss of identity if the child feels overlooked or disregarded. Whatever the 'loss', it can only be dealt with once the angry feelings have been externalised and soothed.

Moreover, it is more effective when the angry feelings are treated in this order: firstly by externalising and then soothing. A good starting point is to consider ways in which the child can express their anger in a safe way perhaps through a breathing exercise or some body work or even a run around the garden or playground. What is not helpful is to continually use repressive intervention which makes the child feel even more trapped inside their angry feelings. Safe expression rather than repression is, therefore, in most cases, much more helpful for an angry child. Once the child has calmed down with the aid of one of the following breathing exercises, mimes or some other safe physical activity, then, if age appropriate, an activity such as *The Volcano* can be used to discover the underlying cause.

Candle Breathing

Note of caution. Restrict the activity below to three or four breaths if the child is breathing in through their mouth, to prevent hyperventilating.

This technique can be used for children as young as three or four if led by an adult and kept very short and sweet!

- Hold up your forefinger for the child to see and explain that it is like a candle.

- Invite the child to try to blow the flame out.

- Ask the child to take a very big breath in (through the nose if possible but very young children may not be able to do this).

- Say they can then blow out through their mouth and see if the flame goes out.

- The first couple of times just let your finger waver like a flickering flame.

- Finally, after an extra big effort let your finger collapse as the flame dies.

- Congratulate the child on having blown out the flame.

My Candle

- Hold your first finger up in front of you and imagine it's the flame of a candle.

- Let's pretend we are going to try and blow it out like a real flame.

- If you can, take a really big breath in through your nose and hold it for one second.

- Then blow your breath out as hard as you can through your mouth.

- Maybe the first time you do this your finger just flickers like the flame of a candle would, but it doesn't go out. It stays upright.

- Let's try this once or twice more.

- Well done! You have managed to blow out the flame.

- Have you managed to blow out that Big Feeling too?

- You might like to colour in your candle now.

My Candle Drawing

Saucepan Breathing

Note of caution. It needs to be explained to the child that under no circumstances is this activity to be tried with a real saucepan!

*This activity can be used in isolation as a way of releasing strong emotions through breathing or before a discussion activity such as **The Volcano**. The aim is to begin to control the out-breath in such a way that strong feelings are expelled in a similarly controlled fashion.*

- Talk to the child about how it feels to have all your feelings bottled up. Explain that it is rather like a saucepan in which potatoes (or equivalent) are being boiled.

- Ask the child what would happen if you put your hand over the lid and kept it there.

- Explain that this is what happens if we keep our feelings bottled up all the time and don't express them safely or a little bit at a time. (This explosion then usually gets us into trouble with teachers, parents etc.)

- Mime taking the lid off the saucepan repeatedly, allowing the steam to escape safely a little at a time.

- Show the child how to take a deep breath in and then allow the breath to escape as you raise the saucepan lid.

- The last out-breath should be long as you keep the lid raised and allow the remainder of the breath to escape.

My Saucepan

- Sometimes feelings get all squashed down inside us and it feels as if we are going to explode, like a volcano or like a saucepan full of boiling water with the lid on.

- You mustn't actually do this but think what would happen if you put your hand over the lid and kept it there? It would all burst out, in one big rush and probably hurt someone, wouldn't it? Sometimes that's what happens to us. Our feelings all burst out in one big rush and sometimes, someone gets hurt.

- But what if we let them out slowly, like lifting the lid from the saucepan just a little bit at a time and allowing only a bit of steam out at one time. We could get rid of all the steam (and the feelings) much more safely and no one would get hurt.

- Take a deep breath in, through your nose, as big a breath as you can.

- Put your hand out as if you are going to lift the lid of an imaginary saucepan.

- Let the breath out through your mouth in short, sharp bursts and at the same time lift your hand as if you are letting the steam out of the saucepan.

- Keep doing this until all the breath has come out and all the steam has come out of the saucepan.

- Use the picture of the saucepan to draw the steam coming out. You might like to draw how many breaths it took for all the steam to come out.

My Saucepan Drawing

Balloon Breathing

Note of caution. Ensure that all sharp and dangerous objects are removed from the area where the child is going to 'burst' as a balloon.

*This activity can be used in the same way as **The Candle** or **The Saucepan** to help release strong emotions.*

Resources: cushions or soft furnishings for the child to 'collapse' onto.

- Explain to the child that you are going to imagine that you are balloons which need to be blown up.

- To make it more visually real, you could ask the child what colour balloon they are.

- Show them first how they are going to blow up like a balloon by taking some short breaths in through your nose and at the same time raise your arms breath by breath as if you are expanding.

- Ask the child to mime this with you.

- Mime floating around the room together as blown up balloons. (Take care not to prolong this as you are holding your breath.)

- Pretend your balloon is so big it will burst and mime collapsing onto cushions as you let all the air out of your lungs through your mouth.

- The 'bursting' can be accompanied by sounds or movements to show the air (and Big Feeling) being expelled.

- Depending on the emotional age of the child, it can be explained that this is a way of getting rid of whatever Big Feeling they are experiencing.

My Balloon

- Pretend that you are going to blow up like a balloon.

- What colour are you? Can you see this colour balloon if you close your eyes?

- Take some short breaths in through your nose and pretend that you are getting bigger like a balloon.

- You can make your arms go out or up as you blow up like a balloon.

- Hold your breath in for a few seconds as you float around the room like a balloon.

- Suddenly you feel that your balloon has got so big that it has to burst.

- Let all the air out of your mouth and feel your body getting smaller, maybe twizzling round like a balloon does when you let it go.

- If there is something soft nearby you can fall down onto it.

- You might like to make a noise as you do this, maybe like a balloon, or maybe whatever noise your body feels it wants to make.

- If you were feeling angry or sad or worried before, you might like to see if you feel a bit better now as you colour in your balloon.

My Balloon Drawing

Robot/Doll Mime

Note of caution. It is inadvisable to hold the breath for longer than a few seconds.

This activity is based on the stress busting exercise of tensing and releasing muscles which usually produces a state of relaxation and is used in many therapeutic practices. It is most effective if the breathing activity is included.

- Tell the child you are going to pretend that you are robots.

- Ask them how they think a robot would walk; how it would hold its arms and legs; how its face would look.

- Mime how you think a robot would look by tensing all your muscles and walking/ moving stiffly. Encourage the child to copy you.

- Then say you are going to change into a floppy doll.

- Mime, allowing all your muscles to relax, your head to droop and your whole body to become soft. Move around the room as the floppy doll and then invite the child to play with the idea of going from robot to floppy doll a few times.

- Once this has been mastered, see if you can add a breathing technique by inviting the child to breathe in while tightening all their muscles and holding their breath for a few seconds while they walk round as a robot.

- Then show them how to let all their breath out as they relax into being a floppy doll.

SUPPORT MATERIAL

My Robot/Doll

- Let's pretend you are a robot.

- What does your robot look like? How does its face feel? How does it walk? How does it hold its arms?

- Does your robot have a name?

- Take a deep breath in through your nose and feel you are becoming your robot by squeezing up all the muscles in your body.

- Walk around the room as your robot, holding your breath in.

- Then, when you can't hold your breath anymore, let everything in your body flop, as if you were becoming a floppy doll.

- You might like to let your head flop over and your arms to hang by your sides.

- Walk around for a minute as your floppy doll.

- Then practise changing from your robot to your floppy doll a few times.

- How does it feel? Which do you like better: your robot or your floppy doll?

- Colour in the pictures of your robot and your floppy doll or draw your own. If you like you can give them names.

My Robot/Doll Drawing

The Volcano Mime

Note of caution. Ensure that all sharp and dangerous objects are removed from the area where the child is going to 'explode' as a volcano.

*This activity is useful as an energy releasing exercise. It is more effective if done with an energy releasing breathing exercise such as **The Saucepan** or **Balloon Breathing** and then followed by a calming activity.*

Resources: lengths of coloured material, cushions.

- Make a huge pile of cushions and material in the middle of the room.

- Tell the child that this is a volcano and that it is angry; in fact, it is boiling inside.

- Ask the child if they would like to get into the middle of the volcano and see how it feels.

- Pile the material on top of the child.

- Say the volcano is getting hotter and hotter and angrier and angrier. It will soon have to explode.

- Tell the child you will count back from ten. When you get to zero it will explode.

- Count back and allow the child to burst out from underneath the material and then fling it (like the lava) around the room.

- The child may want to repeat this exercise. Allow them to repeat it as many times as it takes for them to feel calmer.

Volcano Discussion

Once a child has acted out being an angry volcano a sufficient number of times and has completed other energy releasing exercises if necessary, depending on their emotional age, they may be sufficiently calm and receptive enough to be able to reason and understand the source of their anger. Cognitive work can then be attempted as follows.

This activity helps the child understand the issues which really underlie their anger and how relatively unimportant happenings can be potentially explosive trigger points. It is a useful group exercise in that it helps children feel that they are not alone with their Big Feelings and that others struggle with similar issues.

Resources: A3 card, coloured pens and sticky paper.

- Draw a picture of a volcano on A3 or A2 card (or use the photocopiable/ downloadable sheet).

- Discuss with the child how the lava rises to explode out the top just like they have done in the mime.

- Talk about the little things which make them angry which can be placed at the bottom of the volcano, those which make them a bit angrier to be placed in the middle and those which make them want to explode, at the top.

- Either allow the child to write, draw or place sticky paper at the various places on the volcano depending on how angry they feel about things.

- This activity can be extended into a class/group discussion on what makes us angry.

My Volcano

- Look at the picture of the volcano. Can you see the lava?

- Colour in the volcano; it gets hotter as it gets nearer the top so you could use a yellow at the bottom, orange or pink in the middle and red-hot at the top.

- What things make you a little bit angry? Either draw or write them at the bottom of the volcano or put them on sticky paper to stick on your volcano.

- What makes you a little angrier? Draw or write these things on the orange or pink middle of the volcano.

- And right at the top, what makes you very angry indeed? What makes you want to explode, just like the volcano? Draw or write about this at the top of your volcano.

- If you are doing this with a group of other children it might be interesting to see what others have drawn or written. You might find they have written the same things as you.

My Volcano Drawing

Jack-in-the-Box Mime

Note of caution. Ensure that all sharp and dangerous objects are removed from the area where the child is going to 'jump out' as a jack-in-the-box.

This is another activity based on the stress busting exercise of tensing and releasing muscles. Encourage the child to curl up as tightly as possible, tensing all their muscles, and then, once 'released', to spring out and stretch as out as much as they can.

- Invite the child to play a game of Jack-in-the Box with you.

- Explain that this is when someone is curled up tightly inside a box and that when the lid of the box is opened, they spring out surprising whoever has opened it.

- Show the child what you mean by curling up tightly on your knees or feet.

- Invite them to pretend to open the lid.

- Jump up quickly yelling 'Surprise'.

- Invite the child to be the Jack-in the-Box and take the role of the box opener.

- If this activity is being used with a class, the children can divide into pairs and take it in turns to be the 'Jack' or the 'opener'.

- Encourage the element of surprise by asking the 'opener' to creep up quietly and the 'Jack' to close their eyes.

My Jack-in-the-Box

- You can play this game with a partner.

- One of you will be Jack and the other will be the opener.

- Choose who will be what.

- If you are Jack, curl up tightly on your knees or your feet and close your eyes, pretending you are in a box. Make yourself as small as possible.

- If you are the opener, creep up very quietly and see if you can pretend to open the lid of the box without Jack realising you are there.

- As Jack, once you feel the lid of your box being opened, you can spring out like a Jack-in-the-Box.

- As you spring out stretch out your arms and legs and make yourself as big as possible.

My Jack-in-the-Box Drawing

The Angry Monster Drawing

This activity can be done with a small group but is more effective if used with an individual child. It is also applicable to other feelings such as anxiety, fear, panic, jealousy etc. It is not suitable for a child in the throes of a tantrum but could be used with children who suffer from repeated angry outbursts when they are in a calm state of mind and able to reason.

The aim of this activity is to enable the child to feel in control of their Big Feelings by externalising them. By creating a monster who is responsible for the outbursts rather than the child themself, it helps to minimise the guilt the child feels which can often add to their distress.

Resources: paper, coloured pens and pencils.

- Tell the child that you understand how they feel.

- Say it's like there is a monster inside them who just gets really big sometimes and has a habit of sneaking up and taking them over.

- Emphasise this is not a scary monster but is just very annoying because it causes a lot of trouble.

- Ask the child if they would like to draw this monster.

- When the Angry Monster has been drawn, the child can then be encouraged to have a dialogue with it telling it how fed up they are with it sneaking up and spoiling things.

- A role play exercise can also be used here (see Part Three).

My Angry Monster

- Sometimes when we are very angry it's like there is a monster inside us which feels like it is growing very big and making us do things we don't want to do.

- This is not a scary monster but it is very annoying because it often makes us get into trouble.

- Wouldn't it be nice if we could stop the monster before it gets too big and makes trouble for us?

- Can you think of a way that you could stop this monster, maybe by catching it out as it tries to sneak up on you?

- What would you like to say to this monster as it tries to sneak up on you?

- Can you draw your monster? What does it look like? Is it big and fierce or maybe small and sneaky?

- Once you have drawn your monster, perhaps you could practise telling it that you want it to go away.

My Monster Drawing

All About Me Book

It has been noted that anger is usually associated with a sense of loss, whether of a person, a thing or a loss of self-esteem if someone has put you down or bullied you. In children this can manifest in sudden uncontrollable rages when some small event triggers this feeling of inadequacy. One way of helping the child to feel whole again and to rebuild their self-esteem is to suggest that, together, you make a book with the title 'All About Me'. The contents of the book can include pictures, photos and writing. Some ideas to get you started are given below.

Resources: pens or pencils, coloured pens, paper or card, scissors, photos, glue, staples and stapler to make the book.

- Favourite colour, animal, football team or player, crystal, pop star, school subject, TV programme, etc.

- Hobbies and interests, etc.

- A timeline showing the child's life so far, together with photos.

- Star sign and character.

- Pictures or photos of friends and family.

The whole book can be decorated in any way that the child wants and then shared with other members of the family or classmates at school.

"And what you can't see and what you can't hear

Just makes you more frightened, it builds up the Fear."

Worry

Although overly anxious or phobic children should be referred to a specialist as a matter of course, there are many children who display a low-level general anxiety which may not be deemed serious enough for referral but which is still distressing for the parent or teacher and the child itself. Furthermore, the fact remains that, even with referral, many such children remain for months on a waiting list while the school or family still have to manage their disturbing and sometimes disruptive behaviour.

Unfortunately, unlike the angry child, the anxious child is not always obvious by their behaviour. Night fears, bed wetting, social withdrawal, nail-biting and school phobia are outward signs of general anxiety disorder but these may not be apparent at school or may easily be missed.

The following is useful to remember when dealing with an anxious child:

- Has the child always been of an anxious nature or was there a point at which this anxiety started? Might this stem from a misunderstanding or event at home or school which could easily be rectified.

- Are the parents themselves anxious about something? With the best will in the world, it is difficult to hide our worries from our children and if unexplained, children will sometimes imagine the worst-case scenarios.

- In the case of school phobia, is it actually school that the child is anxious about or do they perhaps believe that by staying at home they can prevent something from happening? This is often the issue in cases of bereavement or parental separation when the child is afraid the parent will disappear if they are not there.

- Has the child been having any recurring nightmares? These are often a clue to understanding chronic anxiety. An activity to address this is included in this guidebook (see *The Bad Dream*).

- If the child has been showing any signs of an altered awareness for example, disorientation, dissociation or trancelike behaviour or suffering from a hugely curtailed quality of life, then professional advice should be sought.

It is often very difficult to ascertain exactly what is worrying a child. The two assessment activities at the beginning of Part Two may be helpful but often the child does not even know themself. In these cases, breathing activities, especially the following *Golden String Breathing*, may encourage the child to externalise their anxiety even if they cannot put a name, only a shape, to the worry. Thereafter, strengthening activities such as *The Warrior* and *The Lion* mimes or nurturing exercises such as *The Safe Space* or *All About Me Book* can be used to help the child feel stronger and more secure.

Golden String Breathing

Note of caution. It is advisable to limit the number of times this is practised, especially if the child finds it difficult to breathe in through their nose. There is a danger of hyperventilation if done too enthusiastically.

The aim of this activity is to help the child externalise their Big Feelings of anxiety or worry in a fun and creative way.

- Tell the child that together you are going to imagine there's a Golden String coming out of your mouth.

- Invite the child to attach their Worry to the end of this Golden String.

- Ask them to take a big breath (if possible, in through their nose … very small children might find this difficult.)

- Say that you are now going to breathe out the Golden String with the Worry attached and it's going to go far out over the hills/houses/park, etc.

- You might like to discuss where it might end up … on a cloud/in the sea/in the bin, etc.

- Try this no more than three times. The longer they breathe out … the further away the Worry goes.

My Golden String

- Let's pretend there is a Golden String which comes out of your mouth when you breathe out. It is very long and can stretch out for miles and miles.

- Let's pretend that you can attach your Worry to the end of this String. You might like to think about what shape your worry is, and what colour it is.

- You can draw your worry on the end of the String in the picture.

- Take a deep breath in through your nose.

- Hold it while you count to two.

- Then breathe out through your mouth and pretend that the Golden String is stretching far out over the fields or houses by your house or school.

- See it stretching out for miles. The more slowly you breathe out the further out your String will go!

- You could draw on the picture where your String went.

My Golden String Drawing

Belly Breathing

Note of caution. Prolonged breathing through the mouth can cause hyperventilation so this should be limited to a few breaths.

This activity suitable for slightly older children who have better motor control. It can sometimes be difficult even for adults to master this technique which is aimed at deepening the breath and exercising all parts of the lungs. As a rule, we tend only to use the top part of the lungs, breathing shallowly when we are anxious or stressed. Deep, diaphragmatic breathing has many advantages including improving stress levels, the immune and digestive systems among others.

- Place your hands on your stomach just below your rib cage and show the child how to do the same. The middle fingers should be just touching with the elbows out to the sides.

- Explain that you are going to take a really deep breath in, so deep that it is going to make your middle fingers come apart. (With older children you can explain that the reason for this is that when you breathe in your diaphragm sinks down to make room for your expanding lungs and pushes the fingers apart.)

- When you breathe out the fingers will come back together again. (Again, this is because the diaphragm will rise once the lungs are empty of air.)

- It is advisable to aim to breathe in and out through the nose although younger children may find is easier to breathe through their mouths.

- This breathing activity takes practice so don't despair! The tendency for beginners is to pull the stomach in on the in-breath and vice versa. Once mastered however, it is never forgotten.

My Belly Breathing

- We are going to try some really deep breathing which will help us to feel calm and relaxed.

- Put your hands on your tummy, just under your ribs with the middle fingers touching and your elbows out to the sides.

- Take a deep breath in through your nose if possible.

- As you do this, imagine the breath going all the way down through your lungs and making your chest expand downwards and to the sides.

- As it reaches your tummy it will push your fingers apart, even just a little.

- Now let your breath out, again through the nose if possible.

- As the breath comes out, imagine it coming back up from your tummy, through the lungs and out of your nose or mouth.

- Your fingers should now come back together and meet on your tummy.

- This is a difficult exercise to do at first but keep trying and you will manage it. Even a few breaths in this way will help you feel calmer.

The Warrior Pose

The aim of the following activity taken from yoga is to help the child feel strong and able, like a warrior, to resist anything that threatens them, whether this is an intangible thing like a worry or something physical, like a bully.

- Talk to the child about people who are strong and ask them if they have seen pictures of warrior tribesmen going into battle with their spears.

- Invite them to see how it feels to be as strong as a warrior.

- Ask them to stand with their feet as far apart as they can without losing their balance.

- Show them how to raise both their arms to shoulder height and pretend this is their spear.

- Tell them to turn their body to face the direction they are going, turning the feet accordingly to keep balance.

- If they now bend the knee facing forwards, they are in the warrior position.

- Ask them to check that their spears are straight.

- Suggest that they do some deep breathing to help them feel strong and ready for battle.

- You can also suggest they use an affirmation here, perhaps something like, "I am strong. I can do …." This should be in positive and in the present tense. (See Techniques used: Affirmations).

My Warrior

- Would you like to feel as strong as a warrior so that things don't worry or threaten you?

- Let's stand like a warrior and see if it makes us feel strong.

- Stand with your feet as far apart as you can without falling over.

- Raise your arms to be on a level with your shoulders and out to your sides. This is your spear.

- Choose which direction you are going in and turn to face it but keep your arms where they are. You may need to shift your feet around a little to keep your balance.

- Bend the knee which is nearest the direction you are heading.

- Check that your spear is still strong and straight.

- To help you feel strong, try some deep breathing like you did with *Belly Breathing.*

- You might like to give your warrior a name and say, either to yourself or out loud, something like "I ... am strong" "I ...can do ..." whatever it is you want to do.

- You might like to draw a picture of your warrior or colour in the picture on the next page.

My Warrior Drawing

The Lion Pose

Like the warrior the aim of this yoga pose is to encourage strength and courage in the child. As the 'King of the Jungle' the lion is well known for its bravery and fierceness. Encouraging a shy or anxious child to pull faces in this way can help them find their own inner resilience.

- Either sitting on a chair or kneeling, tell the child that you are going to pretend to be a strong, brave lion.

- Spread your fingers wide and hold them out in front of you saying that these are your lion claws.

- Open your mouth wide and stick out your tongue as far as it will go, making your eyes as wide as possible too.

- Tell the child that this is your brave lion face.

- Invite the child on the count of three to be a lion with you pushing the claws out in front of you and making the fierce lion face.

- Then see if the child can show you the opposite face: a frightened, mouselike one perhaps.

- Encourage the child to go from one face to the other: the strong brave lion to the scared little mouse.

- Ask the child which face makes them feel bigger and better.

My Lion

- Why do you think they call the lion the 'King of the Jungle'?

- Shall we see how it feels to be like a lion?

- Spread your fingers wide and bend them slightly so that they look like claws.

- Now open your mouth as wide as possible and stick your tongue out as far as it can go.

- Open your eyes really wide.

- On the count of three let's see if you can do this all at the same time: the sharp claws, the fierce mouth and the scary eyes.

- You might like to push your claws forward as if you were pouncing.

- Now let's see if you can make the opposite face: a scared little mouse. What does this mouse look and feel like?

- Perhaps you could try being a lion and then a mouse a few times.

- What does being a lion make you feel like?

- And what does being a mouse make you feel like?

- Which do you prefer?

- You can now colour in the picture of your lion or draw your own lion.

My Lion Drawing

The Tree Pose

Like the previous two poses, the tree pose is taken from yoga and is aimed at helping the child to feel grounded and connected. When in the grips of acute anxiety or a panic attack the tendency is to breathe shallowly and have whirling thoughts, all of which keep us in our heads. Imagining the roots of a tree helps to connect us to the earth, to our own stable base.

Resources: chairs for balance if needed.

- Any standing pose should come from the strong mountain posture called Tadasana in yoga.

- Invite the child to stand with their feet hip width apart and look at an unmoving point ahead of them at eye level.

- Ask them to imagine they are lifting up the arches of their feet and then their kneecaps. (Very young children will obviously not be able to manage this step.) This will engage their calf and thigh muscles and make their legs feel strong.

- Show them how to roll their shoulders back and tuck their bottom in so that they are not stooped over but are standing tall.

- Invite them to imagine there is a wire coming from the bottom of their back all the way up and out the top of their head. Someone has just pulled on it. Ask them if this makes them feel taller.

- Tell them that they are now standing straight and strong like a mountain and that nothing is going to move them. If you like you could see how strong they are by pretending to push them over.

- Now say that you are going to pretend to be a tree that is not going to be blown over in a storm. Ask them what they think the tree needs to stay upright.

- Ask them to imagine that they are this tree and feel their roots stretching way down into the earth.

- When they are ready, show them how to place one foot against the ankle/knee or thigh of the other leg. They may need to use a chair for balance here.

- When they feel they can let go of the chair, show them how to bring their hands together into the prayer position (Namaste in yoga).

- It might also help to use an affirmation here (see Techniques used: Affirmations) perhaps something like "I am stable, I am strong."

- Extensions for those who can balance are to bring the arms up above the head as if the tree is blossoming or to stretch the arms out to the side as if the tree is growing.

- The important element to stress here is how stable the roots will keep the tree, so the stronger these are imagined, the more easily the tree will keep upright.

- Under supervision the children might like to take it in turns to pretend to be the storm trying to blow the tree over and the tree trying to stay upright. (See Part Three: Ideas for enactment.)

- Alternatively, this activity can be done in pairs with the children standing on opposite legs wrapping their arms (or branches) around each other to help each other to balance.

My Tree

- To be a really strong tree we are first going to imagine we are a mountain since a mountain cannot be blown over.

- Stand with your feet a little way apart and look directly ahead of you at something that isn't moving. This will help you not to wobble.

- If you can, imagine that you are pulling up the bottom of your feet and your kneecaps. Can you feel any difference in your legs?

- Keep looking ahead but see if you can roll your shoulders back and tuck your bottom in a little so that you are standing a bit straighter.

- Now imagine that there is a length of wire attached to the bottom of your back bone and it goes all the way up your back and comes out of the top of your head. Imagine someone has just pulled on it. Do you feel a little taller now?

- Now that you are standing tall and strong, like a mountain we are going to practise being trees in a storm. What connects trees to the earth which help them to stay upright?

- Can you feel your roots going down, down into the earth?

- You may need a chair to help you balance. If you do, put one hand on the chair and place the bottom of the foot that is furthest from the chair onto the ankle, knee or inside of the thigh of the other leg.

- When you feel your roots are strong enough bring your hands together as if you were praying.

- Congratulations. You are now a tree.

- You could say something to yourself like "I am stable, my roots are deep, I am strong," which might help prevent you from wobbling.

- If you would like your tree to blossom and grow you can bring your hands up above your head and then down by your side.

- You can do this exercise with a partner, helping each other to balance. Remember to stand, one on a left leg and one on a right leg otherwise it won't work! Putting your branches around each other helps.

- The more you are able to imagine your roots going deep into the earth, the easier it will be to balance even in the face of a storm.

- You can try this exercise whenever you feel wobbly.

- You can now colour in your tree or draw one of your own, growing, in blossom or in the middle of a storm.

My Tree Drawing

Worry Doll/Puppet

This activity works on the principle that it always helps to have someone to whom you can tell your worries rather than bottling them up inside. Many children will have a favourite toy which will serve this purpose. However, imagining what this toy or doll might look like and then drawing it can be part of the process of externalising the worry. It helps to have drawn and made, as follows, your own worry doll before inviting the child to do the same.

Resources: card, felt tip pens, crayons or paints, scissors, glue, lollipop sticks or other wooden sticks.

- First, if possible, make your own worry doll by drawing it on the card, painting or colouring and cutting out. Fasten the doll to the wooden stick so that you can hold it up rather like a puppet.

- Introduce your doll to the child, giving it a name and saying how you can share anything you like with … Say that you tell it all your worries and that it makes you feel better.

- Invite the child to make their own. You can use the template provided if helpful.

- Fasten the drawing to a stick and suggest that the child finds a name for their doll.

- Play out a short scenario whereby you tell your doll a worry. Depending on the age of the child you can also pretend that the doll has replied by holding the doll to your ear and pretending to listen.

- Encourage the child to do the same with their doll.

My Worry Doll/Puppet

- Sometimes it's really helpful to tell your worries to someone or something. Many children tell their worries to their pet or to their favourite toy.

- We can make a very special doll to whom we can tell our worries.

- You can use the picture on the next page and make it into your own doll by changing it and colouring it. What sort of hair does it have? What colour are its eyes? What is it wearing?

- When you have made it, you can cut it out and stick it on some card to make it stronger.

- You can then use a stick, like a lollipop stick, to attach it to so that you can hold it up.

- What is the name of your doll?

- You can now tell your doll anything you like. They will always listen and just saying it out loud often makes us feel better.

My Worry Doll Drawing

The Safe Place Drawing/Collage

Note of caution. It is important to let the child dream up their own place completely without any suggestions from you. This is so that it feels absolutely safe to the child without anything being included, which may, unbeknownst to you, feel scary to the child. The best way to avoid this is to avoid giving examples but to follow the suggestions below.

This activity is taken from NPL (neurolinguistic programming) and is aimed at providing the child with a safe place to go within their imagination: somewhere which will always be accessible to them and where they can feel secure and protected. Having helped the child conjure up this place within their mind's eye, it is helpful to concretise it through drawing, or, even better, a collage. The more care and attention that this activity is given, the more vivid will be the imagined place.

Resources: pencils, coloured pens, felt tips or paints, scissors, scraps of material or coloured tissue paper.

- Invite the child that to see if they can imagine a place where they feel really happy, where they feel they are completely safe and where no one and nothing can hurt them.

- Remind them that this may be an actual place or it may be a place they have never seen before, which is completely in their imagination. It may be indoors or outdoors. It is absolutely up to them.

- Ask them to close their eyes and take some deep breaths. *Golden String Breathing* or *Belly Breathing* may be useful here.

- Appealing to the senses helps them to conjure up a vivid picture of their place, so for example ask questions like:

  - What or who can you see in your safe place? Is there anyone with you in your safe place? You can have anyone you like or no one at all? Is there an animal with you?

  - Listen really carefully, what can you hear? Are there some sounds which make you feel happy?

  - Is there something nice and soft to touch in your safe place? Maybe something that makes you feel snuggly and warm?

- What about smells? Are there some yummy things you can smell? Maybe your favourite food or just the smell of flowers? What smells do you want in your safe space?

- Remind the child that they can imagine anything they want and that they do not have to have anything in their safe place that does not make them feel happy, warm and safe.

- Once the child has imagined this place, ask them if they would like to draw it, or make it into a collage. Pieces of screwed up tissue paper work really well here to represent the sea, sky, green fields etc and the exercise of screwing up the paper can also be therapeutic.

- When the drawing or collage is finished, you can remind the child that this is a place to which they can go in their mind anytime they feel they need to. It will always be there for them and it will be somewhere they can always feel safe and happy.

My Safe Place

- Wouldn't it be lovely to have somewhere you can always go where you feel happy, safe and secure?

- We can imagine this place in our minds and then draw it or make a collage so that it is easy to remember.

- Take some really deep breaths. Maybe use your *Golden String Breathing* or *Belly Breathing.*

- When you are ready and feeling calm, see if you can see in your mind a place where you can feel really happy and safe. This may be somewhere real or just somewhere you imagine. It may be indoors or outdoors.

- Is there anyone with you in your safe place? There doesn't have to be anyone or there can be more than one person or perhaps an animal? A pet? Or another animal that you like. You are in control of who or what you allow into this space.

- Are there any lovely sounds you can hear in your safe space? Listen hard. What can you hear?

- Feel around with your hands. Is there something nice and soft that you can touch; something that makes you feel snuggly and warm?

- Can you smell anything good in your safe space? Maybe something that makes you feel hungry or gives you a light pleasant feeling?

- Now you have your safe place in your mind, the next step, if you would like to, is to draw or paint it or make it into a collage.

- You can use the empty page to draw or you can use a bigger piece of paper or card to make a collage using bits of material, cut outs from a magazine or screwed up pieces of tissue paper. Tissue paper works really well if you want to give your picture depth, waves on the sea for example, or green hills.

- Once you have made your picture or collage, you will always have this safe place to go to in your mind whenever you feel a little lonely or angry, worried or sad. It will always be there for you and it will usually help you to feel better.

My Safe Place

Go Worry Rhyme

Just as positive affirmations can be useful in replacing negative thoughts, so the repetition of a verse or rhyme can often help ground a child who is overly anxious. The rhythm of the rhyme, especially if accompanied by a beat such as clapping or banging a drum or cymbal, is reminiscent for the child of their very early years: the mother's heartbeat in the womb and the rocking to sleep in a normal mother infant relationship. "Most women rock rhythmically without being prompted, thus establishing the secure patterning of regular rhythms" (Jennings 2011, p. 41).

Any verse or rhyme can be used, the simpler the better and the child can be encouraged to repeat it any time they feel the worry thoughts coming into their head.

The following is an example:

> Worry, worry go away
> Don't come back another day.
> If you come back more than twice
> I'll just think of something nice!

The Happiness Box *could then come in useful if the child has been able to put in drawings or writings of things which make them happy. A sheet is provided for the child to draw something 'nice' which makes them happy. This can then go into the Happiness Box.*

My Happy Drawing

The Bad Dream Storyboard

A recurrent bad dream can be very scary for a child and is often indicative of an underlying fear or anxiety which the child may find difficult to articulate. A skilled therapist can work with this but in the absence of this kind of support the following activity may be helpful in reframing this sort of anxiety.

Resources: pencils, coloured pens or felt tips, paper or the template provided.

- Gently encourage the child to tell you about their bad dream.

- Say that if they would like to, you could see if, together, you could change the ending so that the bad dream would go away.

- If they are in agreement, invite them to help you divide the dream into sections so that you can make it into a storyboard like in a comic or magazine.

- Either use the template provided, or if more sections are needed, design your own storyboard.

- Help them to draw or write in each section apart from the last one which you leave blank. This can be in cartoon form with speech bubbles or just drawing depending on the ability of the child.

- Discuss with the child how they would have liked their dream to end. What would they like to have happened?

- Suggest that they draw this fictional ending in the last blank storyboard section.

- Further ways of exploiting this activity are given in Part Three.

My Bad Dream

- Do you have a bad dream that keeps coming back?

- If you would like to try to stop this bad dream from coming back, drawing it and changing the ending may help.

- You can use the template provided to divide your bad dream up into sections.

- You can either draw, write or make figures with speech bubbles like in a cartoon.

- What happens in the beginning of your dream? Put this in the first square and then continue putting the rest of the dream in the other squares.

- Stop before you get to the end of the dream story.

- Leave the last square blank.

- What would you have liked to have happened in your dream? Could you imagine how the dream might have had a happy ending? Ask your teacher or another adult to help you with this is you are not sure.

- Draw this happy ending in your last blank square.

- You could colour in your story now if you like.

- Close your eyes and see if you can see this happy ending in your mind.

My Bad Dream

The Pink and Blue Room Discussion

Many children have difficulty is distinguishing between fantasy and reality. In particular, but not always, if they have been allowed to watch violent films or subjected to witnessing other violence in the home. The same level of fear may be activated whether the source is real or fictional, and a young child may not be able to tell the difference (see Part One, Emotional Development and Abstract Fear). They may become anxious that the 'monsters' in the films will creep into their own lives. They want to know what is 'true life' as one little girl put it, and what isn't. These children will often tell what appear to be fibs or fantastical stories.

This activity helps the child to tell the difference between what is real and what is not and is most effective if used comprehensively at home and school as in "Is that a pink or a blue thing you are telling me?"

Resources: pink and blue material or cushions.

- Divide the room into two and place blue material etc. in one half and pink in the other.

- Tell the child you are going to play a game about what is 'true life' and what is pretend or make believe.

- Sit on the blue side with the child and ask questions which are about real events such as "What did you have for breakfast?" "Where did you go on holiday?", etc.

- Then move over to the other pink side and ask about the films or stories they may have seen or read. "What's your favourite story/character?"

- Explain that when they have something to tell you they can play the game and decide if it comes from the blue side or the pink side.

My Pink and Blue Room

- Sometimes it's difficult to know what is true life and what is just pretending. Sometimes too, things that are just pretending can make us feel really scared when, really, they are only pretending and not true at all.

- It can help us to think about what is real and what is not if we link these things to a colour: say blue for what is real or true, like what you had for breakfast, and pink for what is only a story or just pretending, like your favourite fairy story or your brother saying he is giant who is going to gobble you up.

- Collect some blue and pink material or cushions and put the blue on one side of the room and pink on the other.

- You can now sit with your teacher, parent or friend on the blue side and tell each other some things you know to be true.

- Then move over to the pink side and talk about some things you know are only pretending.

- You can use the template provided to draw or write in some true things on the blue side and some pretend things on the pink side and colour everything blue or pink so you remember.

My Pink and Blue Room Drawing

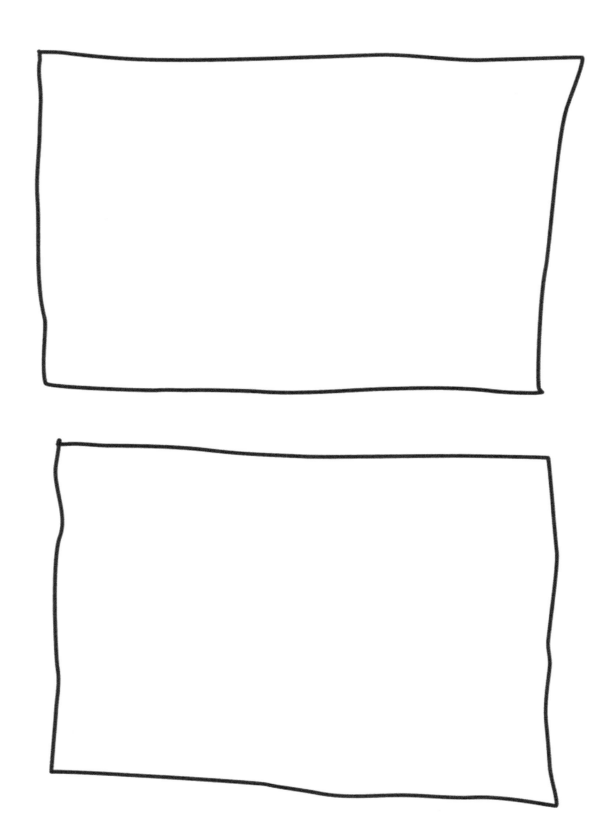

Part Three

In Part Three we consider ways in which the story and activities can be further exploited:

- Through discussion

- Through enactment

- Through puppets

- Through using material to make up your own story about the Monster Elwig

- Through making models

Ideas for discussion

- Why does the King have such a big gold palace?

- How does the Mouse get the King to 'get up off his throne'?

- Do we sometimes pretend to be 'big and strong' when inside we feel very small? Can you think of any times you have done this?

- Why does the Mouse tell the King he's 'getting it wrong'?

- Why is everyone scared of the Monster when they haven't seen or heard him?

- What other things that we can't see or hear make us frightened?

- What do you think of the King? Is he a good King? In the beginning? In the end?

- What do you think of the Boy in the story?

- How does the Boy get the King to go and find the Monster?

- How do the King and the Mouse help all the People?

- How does doing the breathing and all the other activities make the people feel?

- In what way is the Monster Elwig just like the King?

- In the end the King says 'we've all learnt a lesson'. What do you think this lesson might be?

- What do you think Elwig might tell his friends when he gets back home?

DOI: 10.4324/9781003386414-3

Ideas for enactment

Dramatic play is crucial to a child's development. "Through dramatic play a child can reduce the world to a size where it is manageable and where the events of everyday reality can be played out in comparative safety" (McFarlane 2005, p. 8). From a very early age children love to play 'let's pretend' games. It is part of their natural mode of expression: rehearsing 'what is' in the 'what if'. A child will often replay the events of a day or experience that has affected them in some way: Christmas morning opening stockings for example, or a first day at school. I remember my granddaughter after her first day disappearing upstairs to 'take the register'. Joshua, whoever he was, came in for a lot of scolding that afternoon!

So it is through play that children can externalise their emotions. What then, is the difference between play and performance? For the purposes of this guidebook I would venture to suggest simply that performance is witnessed play. Being held in positive, non-judgmental regard enables a child to be themselves, to express their hopes, fears, anger or shame. In a controlled situation when these emotions are not only witnessed but accepted, the child learns that they are acceptable too, in their entirety, both the good and the not so good bits.

Therefore, in order not only to keep any attempt at enactment as safe as possible but to ensure that the child gains the maximum benefit from it, it would be helpful to observe the following:

- An atmosphere of respect for the 'performer' or 'performers', i.e. no talking over, laughing at, etc.

- Adequate time given to each performance or if time is running out the child given enough warning that they will soon have to "bring their story to an end".

- If in a group, avoidance of value judgments on the ability of the performers, since this creates a sense of competition. Instead, the witnesses can make observations about the characters in the story, e.g. "the King looked really scared when he was going into the cave". "The boy (in the nightmare) was brave to stand up to the bully and tell him to go away like that".

- After the performance, depending on the age and ability of the children, a discussion can be held as to how the actors felt playing their parts. Questions should be directed to the children who will speak as their characters, e.g. "As the tree, what did you have to do so that the storm didn't blow you over?" "As the King, what did you expect to find in the cave?" (See Appendix: Speaking from Role).

- It is important to stress that no enactment is about the children's ability to perform. Any comments to this effect should be actively discouraged.

The children themselves might have ideas for plays stemming from the story but the following are other ideas of ways in which to use enactment.

1. **Not so scary stories**

   In a class or group situation divide the children into groups and invite them to think about other scenarios where what seems to be really frightening turns out to be nothing at all. Say their story must have a beginning, middle and end. If the children are too shy to act or speak in the beginning use freeze frames for the beginning, middle and end. (See Appendix: Freeze Frames.)

2. **The Tree and the Storm**

   Divide the children into pairs and let them decide who is to be the storm and who the tree. Once the tree has its balance, the storm must try to blow it over by any means except touching: making faces, blowing, jumping up and down, etc. They can then swap roles.

3. **The Angry Monster**

   Once the children have drawn their angry monster, they can have a conversation with it. This comes to life better if the drawing can be transferred onto a paper plate which can act as a mask. The children can then ask the questions as themselves such as "Why are you always sneaking up on me?" and "Why are you so angry?" and then put on their angry masks and answer as the angry monster.

4. **The Bad Dream**

   Once the child has produced their storyboard of their bad dream with its changed positive ending (see Part Two: *The Bad Dream Storyboard*), this can be acted out either with the child taking part or with the child directing the performance. Being either the main actor or director in the altered ending is empowering for the child since the physical manifestation, in other words the 'doing', is more effective in erasing the original trauma of the bad dream than 'talking' would be – "…many of the symptoms are unconscious, non-verbal, right-brained that cannot, in fact be accessed through talk therapy" (Kellerman and Hudgins 2000, p.12).

   The Freeze Frame technique (see Appendix) can be employed here to start the enactment off and the Speaking from Role (Appendix) to deepen the awareness of the now positive ending to the bad dream.

Puppets

If the child has not yet reached the stage of emotional development where they are ready to take on role (see Part One: Stages of emotional development), projective work can be usefully employed to further exploit the story or use with the activities. For example, in the *Worry Doll/Puppet* activity the Worry Doll puppet is there for the child to offload their worries but an adult can also pretend to hear the Worry Doll's own worries by putting the puppet up to their ear and pretending it is speaking.

If the adult knows that the child is concerned about something that happened at school for instance, they could start the conversation as follows:

"I think (give the Worry Doll a name, for example, Tilly) wants to tell us something. Do you Tilly?" (Puppet nods.)
   "Is something bothering you?" (Puppet nods.)
   "Is it something that happened at home?" (Puppet shakes head.)
   "Is it something that happened at school?" (Puppet nods.)
   "Can you tell me what it is?" (Hold puppet to ear and pretend to listen. Then say to the child, "I can't hear/understand what Tilly is saying. Can you listen?" (hold puppet to child's ear).) Hopefully the child will then be able to tell you what is bothering Tilly/them.

Alternatively, the adult could say, "I don't think Tilly wants to talk to me, she says she wants to tell you."

Strategies like this are useful if the child concerned needs a little prompting to share their anxiety.

Material

A useful resource is to collect lengths of different coloured material which can be used to transform a room into whatever landscape the child chooses. For the story, lengths of blue and green material for example can become the sea with a length of black cloth carefully placed over some cushions acting as the cave. Yellow material draped over a chair serves as the palace of gold and other coloured fabrics tied around waists or over shoulders allow the children to 'dress up' as their characters.

Alternatively, the whole story can be told just using material without the children taking on roles by imagining that each piece of material represents something or someone different in the story and placing it appropriately while telling the story.

Models

Making models for the characters in the story out of clay, cardboard or whatever other medium is appropriate is another way of allowing the children to further identify with the main themes of the story. Allowing the children to choose which character they would like to make and then asking them why they chose this character and what they liked about them, could be an interesting exercise. Is it the resourceful little Mouse, or the dippy King who turns up trumps in the end, or the brave Boy, or perhaps even Elwig himself who, is different inside from how he appears on the outside. If appropriate, some positive comments could be made about the choices made by the children. For example, "You have plenty of ideas about things too, like the little Mouse, don't you?" Or "You're really quite brave too, aren't you." Commenting on the choices should obviously only be done in the spirit of giving the child confidence or raising their self-esteem and not laboured if it does not feel natural.

Appendix

Appendix

The following activities and exercises can be used in connection with the Elwig story itself or with any other enactment involving managing Big Feelings. Advice for the safe handling of these therapeutic drama activities is given in Part Three: Ideas for Enactment and should be strictly followed by the group leader.

Freeze Frames

Note of caution. Children need to be at a stage of emotional development (see Part One: Stages of emotional development) when they are capable of empathy i.e. can see themselves as others see them before attempting this exercise.

The aim of this activity is to encourage children who are reluctant to engage in role-play and to give a starting point for the enactment.

- Start with a familiar scene such as a wedding, football match or Christmas family dinner and ask the children to tell you who might be at such a scene.

- Ask for volunteers to come and stand in the positions of the leading characters; for example, the bride, groom, goal scorer, etc.

- Ask the children to stand how they think their characters might be standing and if their bodies can show how they might be feeling.

- See if the characters can show how they are feeling with their faces too.

- Once the children understand how freeze frames work, take a familiar fairy story, for example, and ask them to show you a freeze frame for the beginning, middle and end of the story. This could be done by dividing a class into different groups and choosing different fairy stories, each group then having to try to guess which story was being depicted.

- This technique can then be used for any enactment in which the children wish to engage and the story can gradually evolve by moving from one freeze frame to the next. This structure is usually dispensed with when the children gain more confidence.

Speaking from Role

Note of caution. Children need to be at a stage of emotional development (see Part One: Stages of emotional development) when they are capable of empathy i.e. can see themselves as others see them before attempting this exercise.

The aim of this activity is to help the children understand why people have certain reactions and do certain things as well as normalising and accepting the Big Feelings which motivate these actions. It should always be carefully structured and led by the adult.

- After a role play ask the children in the acting group to remain in role and invite questions from the rest of the group.

- These questions should **not** be about the performance but about the feelings of the characters. For example, "Elwig, how did you feel when you were discovered?" "King, what made you decide to listen to Mouse?"

- This should be strictly monitored and examples given by the adult before allowing the children free range over the questions.

- Give each character time to reply but stress they do not have to think too deeply about the answer: the first answer being probably the nearest to the truth.

- Make sure each character de-roles after this activity.

De-roling

The aim of this exercise is to ensure that everyone returns to their normal activities without residual emotions which might not belong to them but to the characters they were playing.

- Ask the actors to stand in a circle with a little space between them.

- Ask them one by one to pretend they are taking off the 'cloak' of their character and throwing in into the centre of the circle.

- As they take off their 'cloak' they can say "I am not … (the character). I am (their name)."

- The power of this exercise lies in the witnessing as each member of the group does this individually.

- If the enactment has aroused some strong feelings, the children can stamp their feet as they take off their 'cloaks' and add something about themselves for example, "I am Maria and I have a dog called Freddy."

References

Bradbury-Jones C., and Isham L. (2020) 'The pandemic paradox: The consequences of COVID-19 on domestic violence.' *Journal of Clinical Nursing 29*(13–14), 2047–2049.

Casson, J. (1998) 'Right/left brain and dramatherapy'. *Dramatherapy Journal 20*(Spring),14.

Cattanach, A. (1994) 'The Developmental Model of Dramatherapy', in S. Jennings, A. Cattanach, S. Mitchell, and A. Chesner (eds), *The Handbook of Dramatherapy*. London: Routledge.

Chown, T. (2013) 'When the child proof cap has been left off the medicine bottle – Dramatherapy with young people affected by parental drug and alcohol problems.' *Dramatherapy Journal 35*(3).

Erikson, E.H. (1959) *Identity and the Life Cycle*. Psychological Issues Monograph. New York: International Universities Press.

Jennings, S (2011) *Healthy Attachments and Neuro-Dramatic Play*. London: Jessica Kingsley.

Kelleher, L. (2021, 31 January) 'Mental health tsunami' as children struggle with lockdowns. Available at: https://www.independent.ie/irish-news/news/mental -health-tsunami-as-children-struggle-with-lockdowns-40031590.html (accessed 18 March 2022).

Kellerman, P.F., and Hudgins, M.K. (2000) *Psychodrama with Trauma Survivors: Acting Out Your Pain*. London: Jessica Kingsley.

Lahad, M. (2000) *Creative Supervision. The Use of Expressive Arts in Supervision and Self-supervision*. London: Jessica Kingsley.

McFarlane, P. (2005) *Dramatherapy: Developing Emotional Resilience*. London: David Fulton.

McFarlane, P. (2012) *Creative Drama for Emotional Support*. London: Jessica Kingsley.

Piaget, J. (1970) 'Piaget's Theory', in P.H. Mussen (ed.), *Carmichael's Manual of Child Psychology*, Volume 1. New York: John Wiley.

Sunderland, M. (2006) *The Science of Parenting*. London: Dorling Kindersley.

The Olympic State of Mind Channel. Available at: https://olympics.com/en/video/can -imagining-success-actually-help-you-achieve-it-olympic-state-of-mind (accessed on 30 June 2022).